Soul Therapy

MY HEARTBEAT

KID HAITI

BALBOA.PRESS

A DIVISION OF HAY HOUSE

Balboa Press books may be ordered through booksellers or by contacting:

Balboa Press
A Division of Hay House
1663 Liberty Drive
Bloomington, IN 47403
www.balboapress.com
844-682-1282

Print information available on the last page.

ISBN: 979-8-7652-4043-4 (sc)
ISBN: 979-8-7652-4096-0 (e)

Library of Congress Control Number: 2023906479

Balboa Press rev. date: 04/20/2023

I FELT TEARS OF JOY, I KNELT IN FEAR CAUSE I COULD HAVE BEEN DESTROYED, I ROSE UP I DIDN'T FAINT, ONLY CHRIST KNOWS MY STRENGTH, I DON'T WALK IN EVIL, I TALK CAUSE WE EQUAL, I CAN'T PARTAKE IN THE FILTH, THEIR HEART BREAKS WITH GUILT, TRANSFORM UNDER THAT PRESSURE, CAN'T BE LUKEWARM WHEN SIN IS THE MEASURE, WHEN YOU FEEL GOOD, YOU HEAL GOOD, GOT TO DO THE WILL OF GOD, EVEN WHEN IT FEELS HARD, I CAN MAKE HER SMILE,

DON'T FORSAKE ME I'M YOUR CHILD, KEEP YOUR FAITH I KNOW IT'S BEEN A WHILE.

THE BEAST REBUKED, THEY TRYING TO NUKE THE STREETS, CHRIST IS MY PEACE, HAD TO REGAIN CLARITY, THRU THE PAIN MY HEART WAS IN CHARITY, NO FEAR IN MY VEINS THEY AIN'T SCARING ME, THE WORLD IS IN DANGER MODE, EVERYWHERE I GO FEEL LIKE A STRANGER KNOW, THE LAMB'S SUPPER, I'LL ALWAYS LOVE HER, SEE THE PAIN OF THE EARTH,

RUNNING THRU THE VEINS OF THE EARTH, REPENTANCE IS KEY, WE DANCING WITH THE TREES, CAN'T TAKE NO DEAL, CAN'T FAKE HOW I FEEL, THIS IS DEEPER THAN MUSIC, BETTER KEEP IT OR YOU LOSE IT, 4TH AND INCHES NO EXCUSES.

STAY PRAYED UP, GET YOUR WEIGHT UP, KEEP YOUR VOWS TO GOD, THEY ACT FOUL WHEN THEY SEE YOUR HEART, WHEN THE DAYS WERE TROUBLE, KEPT MY WAYS HUMBLE, VICTORY IN CHRIST MYSTERY IN THE LIGHTS, I'M

IN A DIFFERENT LANE, WITH A GIFT OF PAIN, I CAN STILL SMILE, CAUSE I KNOW I'M GOD'S CHILD, STRENGTH BEYOND MEASURE, I TRAINED BEYOND PRESSURE, TRUE REDEMPTION PUT ME IN A NEW DIMENSION.

FUELED BY A PURPOSE, AIN'T FOOLED BY THE WORSHIP, MY SOUL AIN'T FOR PURCHASE, I KNOW WHERE THE EARTH IS, THE BREAD FEED US, I SAID HIS NAME IS JESUS, WHY DON'T THEY BELIEVE US, PRAYING FOR A MIRACLE, WE AIN'T PLAYING THIS IS CRITICAL,

MEMORIES IN THE CHOIR, ENERGY ON FIRE, I GIVE YOU A REASON, GOD MADE YOU FOR THIS SEASON, THERE'S HOPE IN YOUR EYES, JUST OPEN YOUR EYES.

A LOT OF PAIN, SWEAT AND FEAR, IN THE RAIN COULDN'T FORGET THE YEARS, THE NIGHTMARES THAT I SEEN, THE RIGHT PRAYERS THAT I DREAMED, FEEL LIKE A MOTION PICTURE, FEEL LIKE THE OCEAN IS SCRIPTURES, YOU GOTTA KNOW WHAT'S AT STAKE, YOU GOT TO LIVE IN CHRIST FOR GOD'S SAKE, MY WAYS BEEN CORRECTED,

MY DAYS BEEN PROTECTED, GREET ME FROM THE HEART, MEET ME FROM THE HEART, THIS LOVE IS BEAUTIFUL, ONLY DOVES AT THE EARTH'S FUNERAL.

IT'S A BRAND NEW DAY, IN THE LAND WHERE I PRAY, NO MAKEUP FOR THE FLOWER, WAKE UP WITH THE POWER, THE LAMB OF GOD, THE HAND OF GOD, WE CLAIM CHRIST IN OUR HEART, AIN'T NO GAME WHEN THE PRICE IS FOR YOUR HEART, THE STREETS IS COLD, BUT ONE DAY THE STREETS WILL BE GOLD, GOT TO BUILD ONE ANOTHER,

BE REAL WITH ONE ANOTHER, WHAT I'M DESTINED TO BE ONLY GOD KNOWS, WHEN I REST IN PEACE ONLY MY HEART KNOWS.

THIS IS THE FINAL TESTAMENT, I PRAY MY HEART IS HEAVEN SENT, TODAY IS THE ONLY EVIDENCE, CAN'T PLAY WITH THE REALEST SIN, JESUS IS MY MEDICINE, GLORY TO THE HIGHEST, THERE'S VICTORY IN THE SILENCE, THERE'S A MYSTERY IN THE GUIDANCE, I SEE THE RESULTS IN THE WORK, WE THE SALT OF THE EARTH,

BEAR IN MIND, WE'RE CHANGING THE PARADIGM, SHE'S AN ANGEL ON HEAVEN'S TIME, AIN'T NO FAME AND GOLD, I CLAIM MY SOUL.

THEY THOUGHT THEY RUINED ME, GOD SAID IT'S YOU AND ME, I KNOW IT'S HARD BUT THIS AIN'T NEW TO ME, I DON'T FEAR WHAT THEY COULD DO TO ME, I WON'T SIGN TO ILLUMINATI, KEEP MY MIND FREE LIKE KARATE, MY HEART IN JESUS, IS MY ONLY REASON, THAT'S WHY I'M STILL BREATHING, IT'S REAL WHEN YOUR MOTHER'S

MOURNING, SEE THRU THE MIRAGE, I AIN'T DOWN WITH NO MASONIC LODGE, FIGHT FOR A CAUSE, LIGHT FOR THE STARS, SEE THRU THE MATRIX, WE KNEW THIS WAS ANCIENT.

I GOT A FIRE IN ME, I GOT THE CHOIR WITH ME, STAY MOTIVATED, THEY OVERRATED, I WAS DEALT THESE CARDS, WATCH HOW I MELT THESE FRAUDS, I WAS WRONG WONDERING ABOUT THE ODDS, NOW I KNOW THE LONGSUFFERING OF GOD, FAITH IN CHRIST KEPT ME ALIVE, SEE THE HATE

IN THEIR EYES CAUSE I SURVIVED.

DREAM UNTIL YOU CAN'T SLEEP NO

MORE, THEY SCHEME UNTIL THEY

CAN'T SLEEP NO MORE. GOT TO CARRY

THE WEIGHT, GOT TO BURY THE HATE,

THIS IS MOTIVATION FOR THE NATION.

CAN'T BE AFRAID OF THE MOON,

HANDS PRAYED TO THE NOON, I KNOW

THEY STAYED TOO SOON, DIFFERENT

AVENUE, HEAVEN'S REVENUE, SEEDS

OF INCEPTION, DEEDS OF INTENTION,

THESE ARE INVENTION, HAD TO

CALCULATE, THEY MAD WHEN YOU

ACCURATE, NO MORE FEAR I'M A LAUGH AGAIN, NO MORE TEARS FEEL THE WRATH AGAIN, THE MONEY BEEN COUNTED, THE HONEY KEEP ME GROUNDED, KEEP MY HEART IN GOD, IT STARTS WHEN YOU REALIZE YOU CAN FACE THE ODDS.

THE WORLD IS IN SEARCH, MY WORK IS IN THE CHURCH, MY LIFE IS IN GOD'S HANDS, MY WIFE IS IN GOD'S PLAN, MY FAITH GETTING STRONGER, THE HATE I'M GON CONQUER, HEADED TO THE MOUNTAIN TOP, THEY DREAD ME

CAUSE THE DOUBTING STOP, THIS IS BEYOND RECOGNITION, THIS IS THE DAWN TO CHECK YOUR CONDITION, WE DON'T DEAL WITH SUPERSTITION, KEEP IT REAL WE AIN'T WISHING, SEE FROM THE HEART, WE'VE BEEN FREE FROM THE START.

AIN'T NO BAILOUTS, AIN'T NO FAIL OUTS, I DON'T NEED NO HANDOUTS, I ALREADY STAND OUT, MY FAITH IS IN GOD, I FEEL GREAT AGAINST THE ODDS, BE REAL EVEN WHEN LIFE IS HARD, I SEEN WHAT THE WORLD

DO, I JUST HOPE THEY HEARD YOU, NO MORE EXCUSES, TELL FAILURE DEUCES, IN THE FACE OF ADVERSITY, I GOT GRACE IN THE VERSE IN ME, I AIN'T HERE FOR THE DIAMONDS AND PEARLS, NO MORE FEAR OF DYING IN THE WORLD, I HEAR THE CRYING OF THE BIRDS, THE PAIN AIN'T OVER, THE RAIN KEEP ME SOBER, ROSE OF THE CONCRETE, SOULS OF THE HEART MEET.

LIFE IS THE TRUE BREATH, THERE'S ONLY A FEW LEFT, THIS GENERATION

IS DEAF, THERE'S ONLY A FEW GOD
FEARING PEOPLE LEFT, DON'T FEAR
SUCCESS, PUSH YOURSELF TO BE THE
BEST, CHRIST IS WHAT I CONFESS,
I CAN'T SETTLE FOR LESS, GOT TO
GROW IN THIS WALK, GOT TO GLOW
IN THE DARK, GOT TO KNOW WHEN
TO TALK, KEEP THAT HARMONY,
THEIR SCHEMES AIN'T HARMING
ME, MARK OF THE BEAST WARNING,
HEART OF THE STREETS MOURNING,
GRACE AND SERENITY, IN THE FACE
OF ETERNITY.

SO MUCH IS GOING ON, MAKE SURE PEACE IS YOUR SONG, I KNOW THE MARK OF THE BEAST IS SO WRONG, IN MY HEART THE BEAT IS SO STRONG, FEEL LIKE THE DRUM OF THE MOTHERLAND, WHEREI'M FROM YOU GOT TO UNDERSTAND, READING PSALMS WHEN THE THUNDER LANDS, SALVATION IS MY CULTURE, CELEBRATION FOR THE ULTRA, DIVINE REMEDY, DEFINE ENERGY, FEEL LIKE AN OUTCAST, THERAPY IN A PODCAST, THERE WAS FEAR IN THE NIGHTS OF

SHAME, I DON'T CARE ABOUT THE LIGHTS OF FAME, KEEP MY INTEGRITY UNTIL ETERNITY, BE SURE THEY'RE AIN'T NO GUARANTEE.

THE COSMIC LAWS ARE GOLD, IN A WORLD DEPOSITED OF LOST GOLD, LIKE REALLY WHAT'S THE COST OF GOLD, IN A WORLD OF SCIENCE, MY ONLY WORD IS SILENCE, KEEP GOD NEAR TO ME, DEEP WITHIN THEY AIN'T NO FEAR IN ME, I HOPE THEY HEARING ME, SEE THE SCOPE WITH THE GEAR IN ME, ADVANCE IN THE STORM, WATCH

MY PLANS TRANSFORM, ELEVATED MY THOUGHTS, CELEBRATED MY HEART, THIS IS SPIRITUAL WARFARE, THIS IS A MIRACLE FOR THE WORLD.

CAN'T PUT ME IN ANY BOX, STILL BREAK THE COMBINATION TO ANY LOCK, IT'S AN ABOMINATION HOW THEY TALK, MY FRUITS OF MY LABOR, THE TRUTH TURN THE DUST TO VAPOR, WRITE A LETTER TO MY PAST, LIGHT AS A FEATHER IN THE GRASS, IN THE NIGHT THE WEATHER IS MY CLASS, DOUBLE CUP OF THAT ORDER, I KNOW

WHAT'S UP WITH THE NEW WORLD ORDER, I KNOW MY NAME WRITTEN IN THE STARS, IT AIN'T NO GAME ON THE CROSS, IT'S BEEN A LONG TIME COMING, IT'S BEEN A STRONG TIME RUNNING, HER LOVE IS ABSOLUTELY STUNNING, IT'S A MIRACLE WE AIN'T FRONTING.

THE WORD IS MY MEDICINE, CAUSE THE WORLD IS DYING IN SIN, THE BIRDS ARE CRYING IN THE WIND, GOT TO REWRITE THE BOOKS, KEEP YOUR LIGHT CAUSE THEY KNOW HOW TO

COOK, I MEAN IN THE KITCHEN, IT'S DEEPER THAN RELIGION, THE REAPER GOT THEM SWITCHING, THE BEEPER GOT THEM GLITCHING, THEY SAY ERROR CONNECTION, I'M PRAYING FOR HEAVEN'S PROTECTION.

IT'S PSYCHOLOGICAL WARFARE, BUT THEY CLAIM IT'S ASTROLOGICAL WARFARE CAUSE OF MORE FEAR, SEE THE REFLECTION, KEY TO DECEPTION, THE THOUGHTS WE MENTION, THE HEART'S INVENTION, IKNOW IT'S HARD WHEN YOU GOT

TO KEEP CAUTION, JUST KNOW GOD IS ALWAYS WATCHING, THERE'S A DEEPER MEANING, GOT A BEEPER WHEN I'M DREAMING, REPROGRAM YOUR MIND, SO THEY DON'T MAKE YOU A HOLOGRAM OF THE BLIND, THE CLOTH OF SILENCE WILL CLEAN THE MOTH OF VIOLENCE, CHRIST IS MY GUIDANCE.

I SMILE IN THE FACE OF ADVERSITY, MY STYLE IS GRACE AIN'T NO CURSE IN ME, I CLAP MY HANDS IN PRAISE, IT'S A TRAP WHEN THEY PLAN FOR

DAYS, GOT TO OPEN THE MIND OF THE BELIEVERS, STILL HOPING FOR A SIGN IF THEY BELIEVE US, OUTCASTS OF THE WORLD THEY WON'T RECEIVE US, PEEP THE BROADCAST THEY TRYING TO DECEIVE US, THIS SPIRITUAL WARFARE IS LIKE GAME SEVEN, MAKE SURE YOUR NAME IS IN HEAVEN.

I'M SIPPING ON THAT HOLY WATER, I WON'T BOW DOWN TO THE NEW WORLD ORDER, GOT TO DEAL WITH LIFE, GOD WILL HEAL YOUR LIFE, THIS AIN'T MAGAZINE TALK, THIS

HOW A NAZARENE WALK, LIVE WITH A PURPOSE, THE GIFT OF THE EARTH IS, NO COMMERCIAL FLIGHT, I GLOW WHEN I WORSHIP IN THE NIGHT, THE STARS ARE THE GIFT OF THE LIGHT, BLOOD OF A DISCIPLE, MY LOVE IS MY RECITAL, TAKE IT FOR WHAT IT'S WORTH, YOU CAN'T FAKE ANYMORE ON EARTH, I COULDN'T HAVE PLANNED IT, THOUGHT I WAS UNDERSTOOD BUT I WAS STRANDED, THE PRESSURE MELTED MY HEART, YOU GOT TO MEASURE THE WEALTH OF THE STARS,

THEY SAY THE TIMING AIN'T RIGHT, I SAY THE DIAMONDS AIN'T BRIGHT, THEY PRAY I'M DYING IN THE NIGHT, I PRAY I'M A LION IN THE LIGHT.

KNOW THE DIFFERENCE, GLOW LIKE THE HEAVENS, HEARD A LOT OF CONTROVERSY, IN THE DAWN THEY TRY TO CURSE ME, WOKE UP FROM THE NIGHTMARE, FILL MY CUP WITH THE RIGHT PRAYER, I'M MISUNDERSTOOD BY SOCIETY, MY HEART GOOD WHY THEY LIE TO ME, IT GETS HARD IN THE JUNGLE, ONLY GOLD KNOWS

MY STRUGGLE, ETERNITY AWAITS, INTEGRITY INTO THOSE GATES, PRAY AGAINST THE DEVIL'S FRAGRANCE, THEY SAY EVERY LEVEL GOT THE EQUATION, REPENTANCE TO EVERY CREATION.

THE WORLD TRYING TO FINESSE THE SYSTEM, THE WORD IS THE WITNESS OF WISDOM, WE IN THE SEASON OF HARVEST, THAT'S THE REASON THEY TRY TO STARVE US, BUT I STILL GET MY GRAIN, KEPT IT REAL IN THE PAIN, VICTORY IN MY LANE, HISTORY IS IN

VAIN, WE AIN'T MADE IT YET, FREE UNTIL YOUR PRAYERS ARE KEPT, IN THIS WORLD WATCH YOUR STEP, CAUSE THEY ON THE PROWL, TRYING TO PUT YOU ON THE CROSS FOR POWER.

THIS AIN'T A MOVIE FEATURE, THEY CAN'T MOVE THE PREACHER, I DON'T GAMBLE WITH MY HEART, GOT AMMO FOR THE STARS, STAIRWAY TO HEAVEN, THEY WANT YOU TO STAY AWAY FROM THE REVEREND, I'M STILL COUNTING MY BLESSINGS, WEALTH,

PEACE AND INVESTMENTS, ROSE UP WITH THE WITH THE ODDS CLOSER TO GOD, THE DISTORTION IS THE BEAST, NO EXTORTION FOR MY PEACE, LOVE IS NOT A THEORY, THAT'S WHY THE DOVE'S HEART CAN HEAR ME, NO ONE ON THIS EARTH CAN PUT FEAR IN ME.

THEY THROWING SUBLIMINALS, THEY KNOWING THEY CRIMINALS, I'M GLOWING LIKE MINERALS, I FEEL THE STRENGTH WITHIN, GOT TO BE REAL WHEN THEY CAN'T WIN, I DON'T WALK ON PINS AND NEEDLES, THEY TALK

ABOUT SIN BUT THEY MOVE ILLEGAL, THERE'S A STORM IN EVERY BLESSING, I TRANSFORM IN EVERY LESSON, I KNOW IT'S HARD WHEN THEY LAUGH, I ASK GOD TO DIRECT MY PATH, THE LAST ODDS IS THE AFTERMATH.

IN ALL HONESTY, WE AIN'T PLAYING HIDE AND SEEK, PRAYING FOR THE HEART OF THE MEEK, THE ELDERS BE SAYING THE STARS IS UNIQUE, IMMUNE TO THE NONSENSE, COMMUNE WITH THE CONSCIENCE, I HEAR A LOT OF TALKING, I DON'T FEAR HOW THEY

WALKING, STAY OBSERVANT CAUSE
THEY PRAY TO THE SERPENT, THEY
TAPPING INTO YOUR THOUGHTS BY
THE SATELLITE, WHAT'S GON HAPPEN
IN THE AFTERLIFE.

GOTTA CONTROL YOUR ACTIONS,
GOTTA SUN GLOW WITH A PASSION,
THIS AIN'T SCRIPTED, DON'T FAINT
WHEN YOU SEE HOW IT SHIFTED, THE
ASHES UNDER THE EARTH, THEY STILL
ASKING ABOUT MY WORTH, SEE HOW
THEY RUNNING, I KEEP MY FAITH A
HUNDRED, TO LIVE RIGHT, YOU GOT

TO FORGIVE THE LIGHT, I COULD FEEL YOUR VIBES, ONLY THE REAL GON SURVIVE, THE STRUGGLE WON'T LAST, PUT DOUBLE IN MY GLASS, KEEP MY INTEGRITY, IT'S DEEP WHEN YOU HAVE CLARITY, THEY ON THE WAY OUT, I PRAY I DON'T WALK IN DOUBT, THE WORLD KNOWS WHAT IT'S ALL ABOUT.

I DONE WITNESS, I DONE SEEN THE REALEST, THERE'S NOWHERE TO HIDE, WHEN GOD WILL ALWAYS PROVIDE, THEY CAN'T TAX YOUR PEACE, TELL THEM THRU THE FAX WE DON'T PLAY

WITH THE BEAST, I KNEW IN THE LIGHTNING THE TRUTH IS THE RIGHT THING, NO REPLAY BUTTON, WE PRAY TO BE ABUNDANT, AIN'T NO DOUBLE TAKE, AIN'T NO HUDDLE FAKE, STILL LEARNING HOW TO MOVE WITH PEACE, THEY STILL BURNING THE WOOD TO THE BEAST, THEY PLEAD THE OBVIOUS, BUT ALWAYS NEED AN AUDIENCE, CHRIST IS MY GUARDIAN.

I SUGGEST YOU WRITE A THEORY, I CONFESS WHY THEY FEAR ME, SEE IT THRU THEIR DEMEANOR, I GOT

THE KEY TO THE ARENA, I DON'T BOW DOWN TO THE BEAST, PRAYING THEY CROWN ME IN THE STREETS, THEY IN SECRECY, MY HEART KNOW WHAT THE EVIL SEE, I FACED SO MANY SITUATIONS, I FEEL THE ELEVATION, REPENT IS MY EDUCATION.

I TOLD THEM I CAN'T WAIT, MY SOUL OPEN THE GATE, IT'S COLD WHEN YOU FEEL THE HATE, IT'S GOLD WHEN YOU SEAL YOUR FATE, MAKE SURE YOU ENDURE, HOW CAN YOU FAKE BEING POOR, BETTER WAKE UP, THE

WEATHER MAKE UP, GOD ALWAYS BEEN GOOD, IT'S JUST THE MEANING OF LIFE BEEN MISUNDERSTOOD, NO WORSHIP OF THE BEAST, IT'S GORGEOUS WHEN YOUR HEART IS PEACE, GENTLE SOUL AS I WALK THESE STREETS, WHEN IT'S GOLD YOU GOTTA KEEP YOUR RECEIPTS.

PICASSO WITH THE HEART, THE GOSPEL IN THE STARS, SURVIVED HURRICANES, THEY THRIVE OFF EVERY PAIN, I GOT THAT CUP OF SALVATION, WHAT'S UP WITH THAT VIOLATION,

GOT TO TRANSFORM WHEN YOU WALK THRU THE STORM, IT'S A MIRACLE I CAN PRAY, IT'S BEAUTIFUL EVERY DAY, YOU GOT TO MOVE LIKE YOU IN COMBAT, YOU GOT TO PROVE THAT YOU AIN'T ON THAT, THIS WORLD IS ON IT'S WAY OUT, THAT'S WHY THEY ACT LIKE THERE'S NO WAY OUT, MY LOVE FOR YOU WON'T FADE OUT.

THANK GOD FOR THE DAY, EVEN WHEN IT'S HARD I STILL PRAY, IN MY HEART CHRIST MADE A WAY, REMEMBER THOSE NIGHTS OF PAIN, DECEMBER

WAS THOSE LIGHTS OF RAIN, I WAS LOST AND ABANDONED, PICKED UP MY CROSS NOW I'M STANDING, THEY CATCH YOU IN THE WRONG MOMENT, THEY CAN'T MATCH YOU IN THE PRESENT MOMENT, I AIN'T NO BENCH WARMER, THEY CAN'T QUENCH MY KARMA, DEEPLY REFLECTED, KEEP ME PERFECTED, WITH YOUR HEART SPEND TIME CAUSE WE IN THE END TIMES, TEACH ALL MY BLESSINGS, REACH FOR THE HEAVENS.

MEMORIES THAT MADE ME, I STILL

REMEMBER WHEN YOU SAVED ME, NO DANCE WITH THE DEVIL, I'M ON A DIFFERENT LEVEL, I BEEN THRU THUNDERSTORMS, NOW MY SOUL TRANSFORMED, I ONLY FEAR GOD YOU'VE BEEN WARNED, I HOPE YOU KNOW I BEEN CRYING FOR A MINUTE, I HOPE YOU KNOW SOULS BEEN DYING AIN'T NOTHING HIDDEN, THE WORLD GOING CRAZY, THE DIAMONDS, GOLD AND PEARLS DON'T FAZE ME, ONLY GOD SAVED ME.

WE IN THE SAME NIGHT, GAME NIGHT,

DREAMS OF THE PROMISES, THEY SCHEME IN THE OBELISK, I HAD FEARS IN MY HEART, I HAD TEARS IN MY HEART, ONLY GOD KNOW ME, I LOVE YOU, YOU DON'T OWE ME, I FORGIVE YOU, YOU DON'T CONTROL ME, ONLY THE FEAR OF GOD, I PRAY YOU HEAR ME GOD, I REBUKE THE DEVIL, CAN'T BE LUKEWARM ON ANY LEVEL, HOUSE OF MOURNING, THE CROSS WAS THE WARNING, I'M AT A LOSS FOR WORDS FOR THE WORLD I WAS BORN IN.

DEEPER IN MY RELATIONSHIP WITH

GOD, KEEP THE CELEBRATION WHEN YOU DEFEAT THE ODDS, ANYWAY THEY COULD MAKE YOU STUMBLE, EVERYDAY I PRAY I DON'T FUMBLE, I'M IN A NEW DIMENSION SO I GOTTA PAY ATTENTION, ONE ON ONE WITH CHRIST, WONDERING WHERE WOULD I BE WITHOUT CHRIST, NIGHTS I WAS STARVING, FELT LIKE AN ORPHAN, THIS IS THE HOUR TO WIN AND BREAK THE POWER OF SIN, GO WITHIN SILENCE, THEY KNOW WHEN YOU DRIPPING IN VIOLENCE. IN CHRIST I

KEEP MY BALANCE. IN THE LAND OF THE FREE, IN MY HAND I GOT THE KEY, THEY SPEAKING DOWN ON ME, GOD PUT THE CROWN ON ME, LOOK IN THE MIRROR, WATCH THEM COOK IN THE RIVER, HOLY SPIRIT GOT ME MOVING AT A DIFFERENT SPACE, I KNOW THEY FEAR IT CAUSE THEY FEEL MY GRACE, I GAVE MY BREATH, SWEAT AND TEARS, AIN'T NO DEATH THAT I FEAR, WHO'LL BE LEFT WHEN NO ONE IS HERE.

IN THE LAND OF THE FREE, IN MY HAND I GOT THE KEY, THEY SPEAKING DOWN

ON ME, GOD PUT THE CROWN ON ME, LOOK IN THE MIRROR, WATCH THEM COOK IN THE RIVER, HOLY SPIRIT GOT ME MOVING AT A DIFFERENT SPACE, I KNOW THEY FEAR IT CAUSE THEY FEEL MY GRACE, I GAVE MY BREATH, SWEAT AND TEARS, AIN'T NO DEATH THAT I FEAR, WHO'LL BE LEFT WHEN NO ONE IS HERE.

DIFFERENT CATEGORY, KNOW THEY CAN'T IGNORE ME, THEY CAN'T RICH OR POOR ME, MATRIX GLITCHING LAST WARNING, I AIN'T SWITCHING

THIS COULD BE YOUR LAST MORNING, CARBON FOOTPRINT, SOVEREIGN BLUEPRINT, OPERATING ON A DIFFERENT FREQUENCY, WE AIN'T COOPERATING IN NO SECRECY, NO ELABORATING WE DON'T FLEE THE SCENE, I'M NOT WHO YOU WANT ON A TV SCREEN, BORN TO BE A RENEGADE, MY PRAYERS IS HOW I MEDITATE, GOT THE KEY TO HEAVEN'S GATE.

WE JUMP FOR HOPE, LIKE WE JUMP ROPE, I'LL LAST THE MOMENT, I BLAST MY OPPONENT, NO VIOLENCE, JUST

WALKING IN SILENCE, NO NEED FOR A GUN, NO WEED FOR MY LUNGS, JUDGED FOR ALL YOU DEEDS UNDER THE SUN, YOU GON SEE THERE'S NOWHERE TO RUN, PSALMS AND PROVERBS OVER NONE, THE WORLD LIKE A MORGUE, ANDROIDS AND CYBORG, JESUS LOVES YOU.ORG.

GOTTA LIVE WITH YOUR ACTIONS, GOTTA FORGIVE IN COMPASSION, I KNOW THE DEEP STRUGGLE, THAT'S WHY I KEEP HUMBLE, GOTTA MANEUVER THRU THE MATRIX, I

KNEW HER SHE WAS ANCIENT, STILL
BEAUTIFUL, IT'S REAL IT'S A MIRACLE,
GOTTA BE A KIND SOUL, DON'T BE
A BLIND SOUL, I GOTTA GROW WITH
THE SEASONS, I GOTTA KNOW FOR
THE REASON, THANK GOD I'M STILL
BREATHING, REPUTATION OF LOVE,
THERE'S NO IMITATION OF LOVE,
EVERY SITUATION IS FOR LOVE.

I KNOW MY DIVINE PURPOSE, THE
KNOW THE MIND IS OF SERVICE,
DON'T SAY THE BLIND IS WORTHLESS,
I COULD FIND WHERE THE EARTH

IS, GOTTA BREAK FREE FROM THE CURSES, CAN'T TAKE WHAT YOU DIDN'T PURCHASE, THE WORLD KNOW THE DEAL, THE WORD KEPT ME REAL, THE GOSPEL IS MY LOYALTY, GOD'S SOUL IS MY ROYALTY, THE PROPOSED PLAN IS TO TAKE A ROSE TO THE MOTHERLAND, THIS IS AIN'T HOLLYWOOD, IF I WASN'T SAVED THEN THEY PROBABLY COULD, YOUR RIGHT IN THE WORLD IS THE BE THE LIGHT OF THE WORLD.

I GLOW WITH THE GRACE, CAUSE I

KNOW WHAT I FACED, STOP FEARING WHAT THEY ARE DOING AND START HEARING WHAT GOD IS DOING, WHEN YOUR HEART IS FREE, THE WICKED HAS TO FLEE, THEY'RE FAKE SO READ BETWEEN THE LINES, THEY CAN'T BREAK MY SOUL CAUSE I MASTERED THE SCENES OF MY MIND, I KNOW I MADE SOME MISTAKES, I COULDN'T LIVE WITH MYSELF IF I WAS BEING FAKE, I LOVE WHO I BECAME IN GOD'S NAME, HOW I'M MOVING YOU KNOW IT'S NOT A GAME.

KEEP YOUR SOUL PURE, IT'S DEEP WHEN YOU BEING CURED, FROM THE ILLNESS OF THE EGO, BE IN STILLNESS IN THE MIDST OF THE EVIL, THE GOSPEL IS TO FREE THE PEOPLE, BEEN BROKEN, COULDN'T HOLD IT IN, HAVEN'T BEEN HERE IN A WHILE, COULD TELL YOU STILL IN DENIAL, HOW SWEET IS THE FINEST, MY SEAT IS THE KINDEST, PEEP HOW THEY TRIED TO BLIND US, HOW MANY TIMES DOES GOD HAVE TO REMIND US, JUST PRAY THAT GOD CAN FIND US.

LISTEN TO YOUR HEART ROAR, WHAT HAVE I SEEN THE DARK FOR, IS IT NOT TO OPEN THE DOOR, RICHES OF GOD FOR THE MEEK AND POOR, WHAT MORE COULD I ASK FOR, STARS TALK TO THE GALAXY, TRAIN OF THOUGHT NO TAXI, GIVEN HOPE, GIVING UP, NOPE, TOO TIRED TO RUN, WAKE UP TO THE SUN, THE SOUND OF YOU, MAKES ME KNOW I FOUND YOU.

CRYING IN THE CONVERSE, DIAMONDS IN HER PURSE, THE REST IS NOT THE REST, WITHIN I, I MUST CONFESS, THE

STARDUST BEEN BLESSED, I MUST ANALYZE THE TEST, ENVISION THE QUESTION, THE ETERNAL SESSION, I WALK WITH THE RAIN, I TALK WITH THE RAIN, I REMAIN IN MY LANE, SEE THE GLORY, NOW THE WORLD CAN'T IGNORE ME.

THE CODE OF SILENCE, ALL I HEAR IS SIRENS, THE WIND IS THE PROTECTOR OF DREAMS, THE CLOUDS OF THE STREAMS, PARDON THE MANNER, THE CROWN OF THE BANNER, GOTTA RAISE YOUR VIBRATION, GOTTA TO

GIVE PRAISE IN YOUR SITUATION, WE ALL GOING THRU SOMETHING, I CAN'T EVEN LOOK AND SHE'S STUNNING, EVIDENCE I GOT THEM SHOOK CAUSE I KEEP IT A HUNDRED, HEAVEN SENT SO THE ILLUMINATI I WON'T DREAD, THANK YOU GOD FOR MY DAILY BREAD.

I DESIRE TO BE IN HEAVEN, THE MESSIAH IS MY REVEREND, THAT'S CHRIST OF COURSE, GOD IS THE SUPREME FORCE, PAY THE PRICE FOR YOUR THOUGHTS, WHETHER IT'S GOOD OR BAD, I DON'T THINK ABOUT

WHAT I COULD'VE HAD, THE ROOTS OF MY SOUL, THE FRUITS OF MY SOUL, READING THE BOOK OF ZECHARIAH, FREEING MY HEART WALKING THRU THE FIRE, THE DEVIL APPROACHING WHEN YOUR FAITH GETTING HIGHER, BUT THEY CAN'T GET ANY CLOSER CAUSE I BURNED THE WIRE.

WHAT A DREAD AND TERRIBLE DAY WHEN GOD RETURN, LIGHT THE CANDLE IN YOUR HEART AND WATCH THE EVIL BURN, AND THEY STILL NOT GON LEARN, SALVATION SHOULD BE

YOUR ONLY CONCERN, EVERYBODY AT THE CROSSROADS WHEN YOU GON TURN, LOOK THEM IN THE EYES AND DISCERN, TO GOD MY HEART WILL RETURN, ALL THE BLESSINGS WE EARNED, MASTERED MY HEART I AIN'T NO INTERN, ALL MY LIFE I KNEW IT WAS MY TURN.

THEY TRIED TO BURY ME UNDER THE BONES OF JEHOSHAPHAT, I HOPE YOU REMEMBER WHEN THE ROSES TURN BLACK, THEY CAN'T PUT ME UNDER HYPNOSIS CAUSE I AM WHAT I AM

IS ALL I ATTRACT, THIS IS THE HOLY SPIRIT AIN'T NOTHING AN ACT, I KNOW THEY FEAR IT WHEN THEY CAN'T ATTACK, THEY QUESTION MY HEART, CAUSE I AIN'T TRUSTING THEIR HEART, BLASPHEMY IS OBSTRUCTION OF THE STARS, THEY TRY TO SILENCE ME CAUSE I SEE THE CONSTRUCTION OF THE DARK, WARNING OF NOAH'S ARK.

I AIN'T SIGNING NO DEAL, PEOPLE DYING OUT HERE, CUP OF THAT HOLY WATER, THAT'S THE ONLY THING I ORDER, WHEN YOU GOT THE FEAR OF

GOD YOU CAN DEFEAT ANY ODD, I SEE BEHIND THE SCENES YOU CAN CALL ME A DIRECTOR, SIPPING ON THE FINEST TEA YOU ONLY FIND IN MECCA, AT LEAST ONE HOUR IN SILENCE, THE BEAST GOT THE POWER OF VIOLENCE, PRAYER FOR MY THOUGHTS, NO FEAR JUST CARRY YOUR CROSS, ENDURE UNTIL THE END IS WHAT IT COSTS.

THERE'S POWER IN CHRIST, THE FLOWER OF LIFE, NO ONE KNOWS THE HOUR MAKE SURE YOU RIGHT, THE WORLD GETTING DEVOURED BY THE

NIGHT, THE EARTH IS OURS FOR THE LIGHT, THIS IS DIVINE INTERVENTION, THIS IS THE TIME OF REPENTANCE, RENEW YOUR MIND TO WALK IN THE FIFTH DIMENSION, ONLY GOD, YOU KNEW I WOULDN'T FORGET TO MENTION, LIFE IS HARD BUT YOU GOTTA PAY ATTENTION, AGAINST THE ODDS I CLAIMED MY REDEMPTION, ENDURE UNTIL THE END NO EXEMPTION.

EVERYTHING HAPPENS FOR A REASON, CHRIST IS WHAT I BELIEVE IN, SHE WANTS A WEDDING RING THIS SEASON,

GOD IS WHY I'M STILL BREATHING, I USED TO HEAR CLIMB HIGHER, IN MY TIME IN THE CHOIR, STILL GOT THE CHURCH IN ME, STILL GOT THE SEARCH IN ME, LOOKING FOR THE MEANING WITHIN, GOTTA BOOK OF DREAMS JUST HAVE TO REPENT, TEARS OF A LION, FEARS OF NOT TRYING, FINALLY CAME TO THE REALIZATION, KINDLY FREE ALL THE NATIONS.

Y'ALL CAN'T REALLY FAZE ME, Y'ALL CAN'T REALLY FACE ME, LOOK WHERE GOD PLACE ME, HALO AROUND MY

SOUL Y'ALL CAN'T ERASE ME, ONLY THE REAL EMBRACE ME, RIGHT STATE OF MIND THE WORLD TURNING CRAZY, TO GOD ALL PRAISE BE, THANK YOU TO ALL WHO RAISED ME, THEY TRYING TO BURY MY TRUTH, I'M TRYING TO MARRY HER FRUIT, THE GARDEN OF EDEN, DARLING WE STILL BREATHING.

THEY TRYING TO ERASE MY HISTORY, JUST IN CASE THEY WATCHING MY LAST BREATH IS A MYSTERY, MY ROOTS IS DEEP, THE TRUTH IS SWEET, ONLY IF YOU SIPPING ON THAT HOLY

WATER, I AIN'T TRIPPING IF I HAVE TO BE A MARTYR, I'M AGAINST THE SYSTEM, BREATH OF THE ANCIENT WISDOM, I ALWAYS KEPT THAT VISION, BELIEVE IN CHRIST THAT'S MY DECISION.

NIGHTS I FELT ALONE, HOLY SPIRIT WITHIN I CAN'T BE CLONED, SECRETS IN THE SUN STILL UNKNOWN, MY SOUL THEY CAN'T OWN, THEY REJECT LIGHT IS WHAT I WAS SHOWN, JUDGMENT BEEN WRITTEN IN STONE, ARE YOU READY TO

MEET THE ONE ON THE THRONE, I KEEP A SILENT DEMEANOR, I KNOW IT'S VIOLENT IN THE ARENA, I'M PRACTICING MARTIAL ART WHILE THEY PREPARING FOR MARTIAL LAW, OBSERVANT OF MY THOUGHT, CAUSE I'M A SERVANT OF GOD.

LOYALTY OVER FAME, ROYALTY POURING IN MY VEINS, STILL FEEL THE PAIN, I KNOW IT'S REAL WHEN IT RAIN, WON'T SIGN NO DEAL IN THE GAME, DON'T EVEN TRY TO MENTION MY NAME, I'M A LION WE NOT THE

SAME, GIVE UP EVIL AND RECEIVE THE ETERNAL FLAME, I AIN'T CONCERNED WITH THEY CLAIM, MY SOUL CAN'T BE TAMED.

I TOOK A WALK IN THE RAIN, I CAN'T TALK IN THE PAIN, TEARS THAT I CRIED ONLY GOD KNOWS MY NAME, CAN'T EVEN LOOK ME IN THE EYES, SO I KNOW WE AIN'T THE SAME, SALVATION RUNNING THRU MY VEINS, CAN'T EXPLAIN IT BUT THEY ACTING STRANGE, LOOK IN THE MIRROR THINGS BEGIN TO

CHANGE, I AIN'T CHASING NO CLOUT, I'M ERASING MY DOUBT, I HAD TO FIGURE IT OUT.

THE VISION OF DESTINY, MY INTUITION IS BLESSING ME, WITNESS THE BEST IN ME, WATCH HOW YOU ADRESSING ME, I SEE MY DREAMS COMING ALIVE, BEHIND THE SECENES THEY SUMMON THE SIGN, I HEARD THEY GON DO WHAT, THE WORLD NEED CHRIST'S LOVE, THE BIRDS FLY IN THE SKY ABOVE, OBSERVE THE CRY OF A DOVE, COMPASSION IS WHAT I'M MADE OF,

BETTER STAY PRAYED UP, AIN'T NOTHING MADE UP.

HAD TO SCOPE FOR A NEW LANE, PRAY FOR HOPE IN THAT NEW RAIN, I HEAR THEM TALKING, I DON'T FEAR HOW THEY WALKING, LIVING BY THE VIRTUE, WE DON'T DO NO COMMERCIAL, HOW I'M FEELING IS CONTROVERSIAL, THE WORLD NEEDS HEALING UNIVERSAL, THEY PLOT AND SCHEMING, ONLY GOD I BELIEVE IN, I KNOW THE LEVEL I'M ON, I REPENT AND THE DEVILS ARE GONE, YOU GOT

TO FIX YOUR POSTURE. MY SOUL GON PROSPER.

MEMORIES PHOTOGRAPHED, MY ENERGY LIKE A QUARTERBACK, MY ENEMY DON'T HAVE THE HEART TO LAUGH, MAKE THE ROOM SHAKE UP, FEEL THE TOMB WAKE UP, THEY FLEEING THE SCENE, I'M THE REALEST YOU SEEN, I AIN'T SAYING I'M THE HARDEST, I'M JUST PRAYING I KEEP IT BEAUTIFUL REGARDLESS, I SMILE FOR THE OCEAN, ALL THE TRIALS AND DEVOTION, GOT TO PREACH THE WORD,

GOT TO REACH THE WORLD, TEACH THE YOUTH TO OBSERVE, CARRY THE TRUTH IN THE NEW EARTH, MARRY YOUR ROOTS FOR A NEW BIRTH, THE GOSPEL IS WHAT I'M WORTH.

REVERENCE TO MY GOD, HEAVEN'S IN MY HEART, WRITTEN IN MY DNA, ALL I DO IS READ AND PRAY, MASONIC SECRETS, IT'S IRONIC THEY SPEAK IT, THEY AIM FOR THE BODY, NO FAME WITH THAT ILLUMINATI, THEY SCHEMING WHILE YOU SLEEPING, VIBRATING THAT PEACE, I'M LEVITATING THAT BEAST,

NO DEAL FOR MY SOUL, KEEP IT REAL

CAUSE I KNOW.

IT'S OFFICIAL, MY HEART'S INITIALED,

I KNOW THEY COULDN'T BURY ME,

I PRAY THAT SHE MARRY ME, LOOK

AT THE WORLD I WAS BORN IN,

EVERYBODY JUST MOURNING, IT'S

STILL CLEAR TO SEE THAT I HOLD YOU

DEAR TO ME, AIN'T NO FEAR IN ME, I

DON'T CARE ABOUT THE FAME AND

THE DIAMONDS, EVERYTHING'S THE

SAME IN THE SILENCE, AS LONG AS

YOU DON'T THRIVE, THAT'S WHEN THE

EVIL CAN SURVIVE, THANK GOD I'M ALIVE.

I'M ON TO BETTER THINGS, FEEL THE SONG WHEN THE BIRDS SINGS, NOW THEY GONE CAUSE I GREW MY WINGS, THEY ASKING A LOT OF QUESTIONS, MY PASSION IS IN A NEW DIMENSION, THE WORLD CRASHING CAUSE SO MANY DIDN'T PAY ATTENTION, I'VE BEEN GRINDING FOR A LONG TIME, FIGHTING FOR A STRONG MIND, I'M LIKE A HUMBLE GIANT, I CAN'T FUMBLE I'M LIKE A LION, ENEMIES OF THE CROSS,

NOW THE EARTH DYING, SOCIETY IS LOST EVEN THE TREES ARE CRYING, THAT BAPTISM IS REAL, THEY TRY TO TRAP YOU WITH A DEAL, NO CAP THE ONLY WAY TO BUILD IS TO HEAL, I KNOW THEY STRAPPED THAT'S WHY I WALK WITH THE HEART OF STEEL.

IT'S A BRIGHTER DAY, BETTER PRAY RIGHT AWAY. THIS IS SPIRITUAL WARFARE, EVERYDAY IS MORE FEAR, I AIN'T AFRAID, HEAVEN IS MY FINAL GRADE, GOT TO PASS THE EXAM, NO CASH FOR THE LAMB, GOT TO REACH

THE GLOBE, GOT TO PREACH FOR HOPE, THERE'S A LION IN MY HEART, THEY'VE BEEN LYING FROM THE START, IT'S NOT FLESH AND BLOOD, IT'S THE TEST OF LOVE.

I DON'T TAKE NO OATH OF MASONRY, THEY GOT A QUOTE ON MY SOUL PRAY FOR ME, BORN AGAIN BELIEVER, THE GOSPEL WAS MADE FOR ME, GOT TO HAVE THE DRIVE AND THE WILL POWER, GOT TO SURIVIVE THE REAL HOUR, SILENT WALKS IN THE PARK, GAVE ME BALANCE IN MY HEART, I WON'T SELL

MY SOUL, I'M GON TELL THE SECRETS THEY STOLE, LIVE TO DO RIGHT, GIVE A NEW LIFE, KEEP CHRIST DEAR TO ME, YOU KNOW THEY AIN'T NO FEAR IN ME.

THE BIRDS ARE SINGING, THE WORDS I'M BRINGING, THE TIMING IS RIGHT, THE DIAMONDS ARE LIGHT, NO AUTOGRAPH FOR THE NIGHT, SALVATION IS MY CELEBRATION, CAUSE MOST OF THE TIME WE IN DEEP MEDITATION, TALKING ABOUT THEM SCRIPTURES, EVERY MOMENT WE GETTING RICHER, SHOULD HAVE

KNOW FROM THE START, SEE THE GOOD THAT WAS SHOWN IN MY HEART, ONLY GOD BLESSING ME, TO ALL MY LOVED ONES REST IN PEACE.

I CAN'T MAKE A DEAL WITH THE DEVIL, I CAN'T MAKE A MISTAKE AT THIS LEVEL, I KNOW THEY WATCHING, BUT I AIN'T DODGING, READ A VERSE FROM COLOSSIANS. WE FROM A DIFFERENT GALAXY CALL US MARTIANS, THIS IS A NEW RENAISSANCE, THE TRUTH IS HEAVEN'S SONG, I KNOW IT'S DIFFICULT, GOT TO GET THAT WINTER

COAT, SALVATION IS THE GREATEST MIRACLE, I KNOW THEY HATE WHEN YOU SAY YOU SPIRITUAL, IT'S A BRAND NEW TIMING, IN THE MOTHERLAND I'M SHINING, GOT TO UNDERSTAND FOR THE GOSPEL I'M GRINDING, PRAYER HANDS AIN'T NO DEAL I'M SIGNING, GIVE THE WORLD A CHANCE AIN'T NO MORE HIDING.

HUMBLE ROOTS, DON'T FUMBLE IN THE TRUTH, I AIN'T DOWN WITH NO DEVILS, THEY TRYING TO DROWN ME AT THIS LEVEL, STILL FEEL

THE MICROAGRESSIONS, IT'S REAL WHEN YOU DESTROY THE IDOLS OF CONFESSIONS, NO DEAL IT'S VITAL YOU KEEP YOUR BLESSINGS, THERE'S A HUNGER IN MY PURPOSE, I'M GETTING STRONGER IN MY WORSHIP, IT GETS HARD IN THIS THING, BUT I KNOW GOD IS MY STRENGTH, I GOT A PROMISING FUTURE, I STILL GLOW IN THIS KARMIC ILLUSION, I KNOW THE TRUTH IN THIS GARMENT OF CONFUSION.

SOCIETY IS WALKING ON EGGSHELLS,

INSIDE OF ME I WON'T BEG FOR THE CRUMBS OF HELL, THE LIGHT IN ME GOT THE FREEDOM TO TELL, HOW LONG THEY THOUGHT THEY WAS GOING TO BURY ME, I KNOW THEY WRONG THAT'S WHY THEY AIN'T SCARING ME, SHE'S BEAUTIFUL AND STRONG I PRAY THAT SHE MARRY ME, BIBLICAL LAW FOR EVERY NATION, THEY PERISH FOR THE FALL IN EVERY ABOMINATION, BREAK JERICHO'S WALL FOR THE COMBINATION, NO TIME TO BALL THE

PSYOP IS IN OPERATION, DO YOU HEAR THE CALL OF REVELATION.

OPERATING ON A HIGHER FREQUENCY, I AIN'T COOPERATING WITH NO ILLUMINATI POLICY, VIBRATING ON THE LEVEL OF EARTH'S PRIVACY, MEDITATING ON LOVE THAT'S THE GOSPEL'S ODYSSEY, GOT TO CLIMB HIGHER IN YOUR WALK, GOT TO FIND THAT FIRE IN YOUR HEART, LOVE IS MY DESTINY, ONLY ANGELS NEXT TO ME, THEY CAN'T CONTROL ME, UNDERSTAND WHO'S BLESSING ME,

KEEP MY SOUL IN THE MOTHERLAND SO I CAN REST IN PEACE, PRAYER HANDS WHILE I WALK THROUGH THESE STREETS, WE IN SERVICE PLEASE TAKE YOUR SEATS, THE BEAST IS THE SERPENT PLEASE SAVE YOUR RECEIPTS.

MY GARMENT'S IN PEACE, I GOT A COMMENT FOR THE BEAST, I DON'T PLAY WITH SATAN, ALL THEM ANGELS WAITING. AIN'T NO TIME FOR FAKING, THIS IS HISTORY IN THE MAKING, THE WORLD'S MISERY IS BEING

FORSAKENED, SOCIETY PLAYED THE WRONG HAND TRULY MISTAKEN, WE PRAYED IN THE MOTHERLAND NOW WE NEWLY AWAKENED, WE SLAYED THE BEAST NOW THEY RUDELY AWAKENED, WHAT'S THE OUTCOME FOR THE GAMBLE, HOW COME THEY DON'T BRING THE GOSPEL FOR THE AMMO, WITNESS THE MIRACLE, WISDOM OF THE SPIRITUAL, BAPTISM OF THE SOUL CAUSE THEY FEAR THE TRUTH.

MY JOURNEY BEEN LAID OUT, THE DEBT BEEN PAID OUT, I WAS RAISED

IN THE JUNGLE WITH THE BENGALS, HOW MANY DAYS THEY GON RUMBLE WITH THE ANGELS, CARRY YOUR HEART LIGHT, THEY CAN'T BURY THE DARK IN THE NIGHT, FEEL LIKE NOAH'S ARK GOT TO GET YOUR MIND RIGHT, THEY DEDICATED TO LIVING WRONG, I MEDITATED ON READING PSALMS, LEAVE THE PLANET IN GOOD STANDING, WORSHIP THE BEAST IS WHAT THEY DEMANDING, STAY IN PEACE CAUSE THE WORLD IS THE ENDING, NO PART TWO, KEEP MY

HEART TRUE, WHAT I DECIDED GOT
THESE FOLKS HIDING. VIBRATION IS
THE TEST OF THE BEAST, SALVATION
UNTIL I REST IN PEACE.

MY ROOTS IS IN THE CHURCH, THEY
SAY THE TRUTH HURTS, I PRAY THE
FRUITS AIN'T CURSED, I LOVE THAT
SWEET HONEY, KEEP YOUR RECEIPTS
WHEN YOU DEALING WITH THAT
MONEY, WHAT'S THE PURPOSE, I GOT
THEM NERVOUS, WATCH HOW THEY
OBSERVE US, NO FEAR OF THE SAVAGE,
EVERY YEAR IS JUST DAMAGE, THE

GOSPEL IS MY ONLY ADVANTAGE, GOD'S LOVE IS HOW I MANAGE.

I GOT THE HEART OF A PASTOR, MY HEART'S BEEN MASTERED, THEY START WITH DISASTER, WHAT'S YOUR LEVEL OF DISCERNMENT, THE DEVIL CAN'T STAND THE SERMON, MY MINISTRY IS IN THE STREETS, EVERY ACTION I CARRY THE PASSION, THEY SAY THE SUN GETTING HOTTER, I SAY WE ARE ONE IN THE FATHER, EVERY OCCASION IS A MASONIC INVASION, FEEL THE BRILLANCE, BE REAL IN

FRONT OF MILLIONS, THEY TARGETING CIVILIANS, ONLY GOD KNOWS THE EQUIVALENCE.

ALL THE EMOTIONS, RUNNING DEEP IN THE OCEAN, I KNOW THEY APPROACHING, LAMB'S BOOK OF LIFE IS MY ONLY DEVOTION, I DON'T NEED WI-FI TO TALK TO GOD, I FLY WHEN I CRY IN MY HEART, I AIN'T GOT TIME TO DEBATE, YOU WASTING MY TIME WITH THE HATE, WE DON'T SPECULATE, MATTER FACT WE REGULATE, NOWHERE TO RUN, ONLY PRAYER TO THE ONE.

I SEE HOW THE WEATHER PRAY, HOPING FOR A BETTER DAY, I KNOW GOD GON MAKE A WAY, EVERY NATION CAN SING, THE REVELATION I BRING, THEY AIN'T JUSTIFIED, I MUST SURVIVE, WE AIN'T LOST THE VIBE, I BEEN TO PLACES YOU DON'T WANT TO SEE, GRACE IS MY ONLY CURRENCY, WHAT THEY AFRAID OF IS THE EMERGENCY, I LIVE BY THE CODE OF THE BIBLE, THEY TRIED TO MEET ME AT THE CROSSROAD WITH THE IDOL, DON'T SELL YOUR SOUL THAT'S VITAL, LIFE AIN'T NO FAIRYTALE, THEY CARRY

THE SPELL, THEY MARRIED THE VEIL,
I KNOW THE DETAILS VERY WELL, AT
THE END IT'S HEAVEN OR HELL.

WHAT MORE CAN I SAY, RICH OR POOR
YOU I STILL GOT TO PRAY, DEEP IN IT'S
CORE IT'S STILL GOD'S DAY, KEEPING
THE SCORE YOU KNOW I DON'T PLAY,
THE BIBLE IS IN EFFECT, THEM IDOLS
DON'T RESURRECT, HIGHLY ELECTED,
THAT HOLLYWOOD STUFF IS DIRECTED,
I HAD ENOUGH OF THE GAME, ACTING
TOUGH FOR THE FAME. AIN'T NO BLUFF
WHEN THERE'S NO ONE TO BLAME, I

KNOW IT'S ROUGH WHEN YOU FEEL THE PAIN, STAY PRAYED UP EVEN IN THE RAIN, THIS AIN'T MADE UP THIS IS WRITTEN IN YOUR NAME.

THE NAME JESUS BRINGS POWER, THE PAIN GREIVED US FOR THE HOUR, PERSECUTION IS WORLDWIDE, THE CURSE OF ILLUSION IS THE EARTH'S CRY, I DON'T FOLLOW NO SATANIC RULES, THE BIBLE IS MECHANIC TOOLS, WE NEED BELIEVERS PLANTING SCHOOLS, THERE'S HOPE IN GOD, JUST OPEN YOUR HEART, THIS AIN'T

NO PREVIEW, SEE THEM THROUGH THE
REARVIEW, I PRAY THEY HEAR YOU,
NO MATTER WHAT I DON'T FEAR YOU.

EVERYTHING HAPPENS FOR A
REASON, CHRIST IS WHAT I BELIEVE
IN, SHE WANTS A WEDDING RING
THIS SEASON, GOD IS WHY I'M STILL
BREATHING, I USED TO HEAR CLIMB
HIGHER, IN MY TIME IN THE CHOIR,
STILL GOT THE CHURCH IN ME, STILL
GOT THE SEARCH IN ME, LOOKING
FOR THE MEANING WITHIN, GOTTA
BOOK OF DREAMS JUST HAVE TO

REPENT, TEARS OF A LION, FEARS OF NOT TRYING, FINALLY CAME TO THE REALIZATION, KINDLY FREE ALL THE NATIONS.

Y'ALL CAN'T REALLY FAZE ME, Y'ALL CAN'T REALLY FACE ME, LOOK WHERE GOD PLACE ME, HALO AROUND MY SOUL Y'ALL CAN'T ERASE ME, ONLY THE REAL EMBRACE ME, RIGHT STATE OF MIND THE WORLD TURNING CRAZY, TO GOD ALL PRAISE BE, THANK YOU TO ALL WHO RAISED ME, THEY TRYING TO BURY MY TRUTH,

I'M TRYING TO MARRY HER FRUIT, THE GARDEN OF EDEN, DARLING WE STILL BREATHING.

THEY TRYING TO ERASE MY HISTORY, JUST IN CASE THEY WATCHING MY LAST BREATH IS A MYSTERY, MY ROOTS IS DEEP, THE TRUTH IS SWEET, ONLY IF YOU SIPPING ON THAT HOLY WATER, I AIN'T TRIPPING IF I HAVE TO BE A MARTYR, I'M AGAINST THE SYSTEM, BREATH OF THE ANCIENT WISDOM, I ALWAYS KEPT THAT VISION, BELIEVE IN CHRIST THAT'S MY DECISION.

NIGHTS I FELT ALONE, HOLY SPIRIT WITHIN I CAN'T BE CLONED, SECRETS IN THE SUN STILL UNKNOWN, MY SOUL THEY CAN'T OWN, THEY REJECT LIGHT IS WHAT I WAS SHOWN, JUDGMENT BEEN WRITTEN IN STONE, ARE YOU READY TO MEET THE ONE ON THE THRONE, I KEEP A SILENT DEMEANOR, I KNOW IT'S VIOLENT IN THE ARENA, I'M PRACTICING MARTIAL ART WHILE THEY PREPARING FOR MARTIAL LAW, OBSERVANT OF MY THOUGHT, CAUSE I'M A SERVANT OF GOD.

LOYALTY OVER FAME, ROYALTY POURING IN MY VEINS, STILL FEEL THE PAIN, I KNOW IT'S REAL WHEN IT RAIN, WON'T SIGN NO DEAL IN THE GAME, DON'T EVEN TRY TO MENTION MY NAME, I'M A LION WE NOT THE SAME, GIVE UP EVIL AND RECEIVE THE ETERNAL FLAME, I AIN'T CONCERNED WITH THEY CLAIM, MY SOUL CAN'T BE TAMED.